REAL WORLD ECONOMICS

How
Credit Crises
Happen

Barbara Gottfried
Hollander

+6.73
+1.33
+21.64
+14.83
+919
+3.24
+32.47
+11.02
+2.35
+41
+25.05
+021
+2.42
+5.53
+12.41

FORECL

ROSEN
PUBLISHING®
New York

This book is dedicated to Murray Hollander,
who never believed in spending more than he had or could repay.

Published in 2011 by The Rosen Publishing Group, Inc.
29 East 21st Street, New York, NY 10010

First Edition

Library of Congress Cataloging-in-Publication Data

Hollander, Barbara, 1970–
How credit crises happen / Barbara Gottfried Hollander.—1st ed.
    p. cm.—(Real world economics)
Includes bibliographical references and index.
ISBN 978-1-4358-9461-7 (library binding)
1. Financial crises—Juvenile literature. 2. Credit—Juvenile literature.
I. Title.
HB3725.H65 2011
338.5'42—dc22

2009041599

Manufactured in the United States of America

CPSIA Compliance Information: Batch #S10YA: For further information, contact Rosen Publishing, New York, New York, at 1-800-237-9932.

On the cover: Speculative bubbles, or very large increases in the price of an asset, lead to rising stock markets. But when the bubble bursts, stock markets fall. By 2007, the prices of homes fell tremendously and the housing bubble burst.

Contents

INTRODUCTION

In 2007, the world watched as America began suffering through a financial crisis. In the months and years ahead, the housing market collapsed, banks failed, the stock market crashed, companies lost billions of dollars, and people were left without homes and jobs. When people and companies wanted to borrow money or obtain credit, they faced a credit crisis. Available credit was drying up, and America was in the worst financial crisis since the Great Depression.

According to the *Economist's Essential Economics: An A–Z Guide* by Matthew Bishop, a credit crisis is "when banks and other suppliers of credit suddenly stop lending." A credit crisis means that there is little or no credit available to borrowers. This happens when a new development causes a change in a lender's attitude toward taking on risk or when the lender has less money available to lend.

People use credit to make purchases every day. Adults often make monthly mortgage or car payments. Many students pay for their college education through loans. These are examples of using credit to pay for goods and services.

Using credit to make a purchase results in taking on a debt. A financial debt means that money is owed. There are two types of debt: short-term and long-term debt. Short-term debts are paid back within a year. Paying your credit card balance off in full each month is an example of short-term debt. Mortgages and student loans are long-term debts. They are generally paid back anywhere from one year to thirty years after the loan agreement is signed.

Debt is often viewed negatively. In general, debt that arises from consumable goods and services is considered bad debt. Going on a vacation and eating out at a restaurant every night are consumable items. They are only used once. Many financial experts advise against borrowing money to pay for consumable items. Instead, they suggest setting up a savings plan to reach short-term and long-term goals.

However, some debt can be positive. Good debt increases overall wealth, which refers to the value of a person's possessions. College loans help pay for the education that students need to obtain jobs. If the salary from a future job allows a person to repay the loan and provides financial stability, the student loan was a good debt. It enabled the student to invest in his or her future.

Taking out credit depends on both the amount and the price of credit. Financial institutions make credit available in several ways, including loans. They also charge a price for credit, which is called interest. Both the available amount of credit and its price can change. During a credit crisis, there is a lack of credit because financial institutions, such as banks, stop lending.

CHAPTER ONE
THE WORLD OF CREDIT

Investments are one important reason why people borrow money. When you invest your money, you hope to make more money than you originally had. A home is a type of investment. It is also an asset, which means it has value for its owner. Someone who is looking to buy a home thinks about the cost of the house, its location and size, and how close it is to work and public transportation. A homeowner also looks for a house whose value will rise, or appreciate. An appreciating asset is something that is worth more tomorrow than it is today. When people invest their money, they hope that their assets will increase in value. Then they can pay back the money that they borrowed and earn a profit.

People also borrow money to pay for goods and services that cost more money than they have in their bank accounts. According to the U.S. Census Bureau, the average sales price of a new home in the United States in 2008 was $292,600. Since most people do not have more than a quarter of a million dollars in their bank account to buy a home, they borrow money on credit. This means that they take out a loan to buy a house and legally agree to pay back the money in successive payments, or installments, called mortgage payments.

Sometimes people use credit to buy things that they want, but do not have a plan to repay the money that they borrowed. This leads to people not paying their bills, losing the goods and services that they bought on credit, and making it more difficult to borrow money in the future. In the case of credit cards, only paying the minimum amount owed each month can often lead to credit card debt. Credit card companies charge extra costs on unpaid balances. Sometimes these extra costs add up to more than the original purchase. According to the April 2009 Nilson Report, credit card debt in America reached $972.73 billion by the end of 2008.

How Governments Take on Debt

Federal, state, and local governments also incur debt by borrowing money to pay for their expenses. Governments pay for many goods and services in the United States, including roads, post offices, public schools, and the upkeep of public parks. Taxes are the main source of revenue, or money taken in, by the government. When a government's expenses are more than its revenues, the government borrows money. The amount of money that a government overspends in a specific time, usually one year, is called the budget deficit. If you add the deficits from consecutive years together, you can figure out the government's total "debt." As of the time of this writing, U.S. federal government debt totaled more than $12.5 trillion.

As part of President Barack Obama's American Recovery and Reinvestment Act, billions of dollars were spent on improving and building roads and bridges.

Banks and Reserve Requirements

Banks also borrow money. The United States' central bank is called the Federal Reserve, or the Fed. The Fed requires banks

During the recent recession, American car companies General Motors and Chrysler had to borrow billions of dollars from the U.S. government to keep their operations going.

10

to keep part of their deposits in reserve, or safekeeping, and even sets a reserve requirement. For example, if the reserve requirement is 10 percent and you deposit $100, the bank is required to keep $10 of your deposit in reserve and can lend

out the other $90. This does not mean that your money will not be there when you want to withdraw it. In fact, your money is protected by a government corporation called the Federal Deposit Insurance Corporation (FDIC). But it does mean that banks can use your money to earn a profit, as you will learn in the next chapter. If a bank lends out too much of its money or invests its money poorly, it will need to borrow money from other banks in order to meet its reserve requirement.

Capital for Companies

Companies borrow money for many reasons, including meeting start-up costs, expansion, research and development, and acquisition of other companies. When a company is formed, it has many expenses, such as office space and paying its employees.

It also has to pay for materials to make the products. In the case of cars, the materials would include goods such as steel and tires. As a company grows, its expenses grow. For example, larger companies generally have more office space, more workers, and even higher advertising costs. To stay competitive, companies often have to spend money on research. To help them meet their goals companies may even buy another company. Each phase of a company's growth requires borrowing money.

Making Money

Financial institutions, including banks, investment firms, and government-backed corporations, also use credit to make more money. They borrow money to make investments that will offer them higher rates of return than what they are paying to borrow the money. For example, if a firm borrows money at 1 percent, it will look for an investment with a rate of return that is higher than 1 percent. The rate of return is the amount of money that a person makes on an investment, expressed as a percentage. The rate of return is related to risk. Generally, riskier investments have greater rates of return. This is because a risky investment has a greater chance of losing your money than a safe investment. So riskier investments have to offer a reason for people to want them. This reason is more money, if the investment succeeds.

Taking Out Loans

Individuals, companies, banks, and governments take out loans to borrow money. A loan is a promise that the borrower will pay back the money under certain conditions. The amount that a person borrows is called the principal. The lender also charges a fee for loaning the money, based on the interest rate. This rate determines the cost of borrowing money, and it is calculated as a percentage of the loan. When the loan has been repaid, the borrower has paid back both the principal and the interest payments.

A secured loan is a loan that is backed up by collateral. Collateral is a physical asset that can be taken back if the borrower defaults on (cannot pay back) the loan. In the case of a mortgage, the collateral is the house. If a borrower cannot make his or her mortgage payments, the lender can take back the house. With a car, the lender can take back the car if the borrower cannot make the car payments. Collateral makes lending less risky because the lender can still use the collateral to get back some or all of the money that was lent in case of a loan default. By contrast, an unsecured loan, which is not backed up by collateral, puts the lender in a worse financial situation if the borrower doesn't pay back the loan.

Using Credit Cards

Credit cards are another way that people borrow money. Credit cards allow you to borrow up to your credit limit, which is the full amount that you can charge. This limit is determined by several factors, including your credit history, your financial position, and the likelihood that you will pay your credit card bill. A credit card company also charges interest on any unpaid balances. And credit card companies charge some of the highest interest rates around, up to 30 percent. This means that if

Credit card companies slowed lending during the recent credit crisis. They lowered credit limits for credit card users and became more selective with new applicants.

you borrow $1,000 on your credit card and only pay $100 of your bill, you will owe at least $900 next month, plus the interest payment and other possible late fees, in addition to any new purchases you might make. And if your credit card company charges 20 percent interest on unpaid balances, you will owe $180 just in interest on top of the $900.

Issuing Bonds, Bills, and Notes

Companies and governments can also issue bonds to borrow money. The amount of money that is borrowed is the face value of the bond. The cost of borrowing money is the total amount of interest paid. Bonds are issued for a certain period of time. The maturity date is the day that the bond becomes due and the institution issuing the bond must repay its debt. Once this date has been reached, the bondholder is paid back the amount borrowed, plus interest payments. Foreign countries have been buying a lot of U.S. Treasury bonds lately. In 1998, 13 percent of these bonds were held by foreign countries, compared to 28 percent, or $3.2 trillion, a little more than a decade later. China and Japan held 44 percent of foreign-owned U.S. Treasury bonds in 2009.

The federal government also offers treasury bills (T-bills) and treasury notes to borrow money from the public. T-bills are considered short-term debt because they have maturity dates of less than a year. They are sold in $1,000 denominations. Unlike a bond that pays fixed interest payments, T-bills are sold at one price and bought back at a higher one. The difference between the prices is the profit earned by the person who bought the T-bill. Treasury notes are long-term debts, with maturity dates of two to ten years. Like bonds, they have fixed interest payments.

Depository Institutions

Commercial banks borrow money, but they also lend money. Banks offer many services, including making personal loans, car loans, home loans, company loans, and even boat loans. Since banks are only required to keep a part of their deposits in reserves, they can use the rest of the money to extend credit.

Financial Supermarkets

In 1999, the world of credit lenders changed when the Glass-Steagall Act was repealed. The Glass-Steagall Act was originally passed in 1933, during the Great Depression. It prevented commercial banks from carrying out investment banking transactions. When the Glass-Steagall Act was repealed, this restriction no longer existed. Companies were now allowed to offer banking services, investment services, and insurance services. This led to the establishment of financial supermarkets. American Express is an example of a financial supermarket. Such companies could offer credit in many ways, such as mortgages, company loans, and bonds. They could also offer borrowers ways to invest the money borrowed from them. American International Group, Inc. (also known as AIG) is another example of a financial supermarket that provides many kinds of financial services to individuals and companies throughout the world.

Both banks and savings and loans are considered depository institutions. This means that most of the money that they have comes from deposits, or money that is put into accounts. Credit unions, which are another kind of depository institution, generally offer lower interest rates on loans than commercial banks. But you or your parents have to belong to the organization that is associated with the credit union in order to use its services.

Credit Card Companies

Companies that issue credit cards include banks, stores, and financial supermarkets. The most popular banks that offer credit cards are JPMorgan Chase & Company, Bank of America, and Citibank. Discover, Capital One, and Target credit cards are also widely used forms of credit. When you go to a store, you may notice a sign that tells you which credit cards are accepted forms of payment. This means that you can borrow money with those credit cards to pay for your purchases in that store. Usually, stores will accept Visa, MasterCard, American Express, or Discover.

The Government and the Federal Reserve

The government lends money to individuals, companies, and other governments. The Web site GovLoans.com discusses many government loans that are available for education and housing and to farmers, war veterans, and those suffering from natural disasters. According to the College Board, the government gave out $1.1 billion in Perkins loans for college students in 2007–2008. And in June 2009, Bloomberg News reported that "government-insured home loans jumped to 36 percent of all U.S. mortgage applications." A government can lend money to its citizens. But it can also lend money to the

There are 172 central banks in the world. The U.S. central bank is called the Federal Reserve and is located in Washington, D.C.

governments of other countries. When both the Chinese and Japanese governments buy U.S. Treasury bonds, the United States is borrowing money from China and Japan.

The United States' central bank, the Federal Reserve, is  called "the lender of the last resort." When banks need money and no one else is willing to lend it to them, the Federal Reserve will extend credit. According to the Times Online, banks borrowed a record $367.8 billion per day from the Federal Reserve during the week ending October 1, 2008.

CHAPTER TWO

CAUSES OF A CREDIT CRISIS

There are credit borrowers and credit lenders. Together, they form a credit cycle that involves lending and borrowing money. There are periods of time when lenders offer more credit, and there are times when lenders offer less credit. When there is more credit available, the cycle is in an expansion phase. When there is less credit available, the cycle is in a contraction phase.

Understanding the Credit Cycle

Commercial bank loans can help you understand the credit cycle. Remember your $100 deposit with a 10 percent reserve requirement? This example showed that the bank kept $10 in reserve and could loan out $90. A person who took out a loan from the bank might then spend the $90 to buy clothes. The owner of the clothes shop could then take the $90 and deposit it in her bank account. Then her bank would keep 10 percent of the $90, or $9 in reserves, and loan out the other $81. This process of lending and borrowing continues and forms a credit cycle. In real life, many people deposit their money in banks, and therefore banks have a lot of money to lend out.

Why do banks make loans? Banks make loans to earn profit. Interest payments are the cost of borrowing money. They are also the amount of money earned by the lender. If a bank charges an annual interest rate of 5 percent and a borrower takes out a $100,000 loan for twenty years, the bank would make almost $60,000 over the twenty years in interest just on that loan. The more loans the banks offer, the

Equifax (http://www.equifax.com, shown here), Experian, and TransUnion are the three major credit reporting agencies. They provide information on a person's credit history and help deal with identity theft.

more profits they can earn. But a lender's chance to earn a profit is related to the ability of the borrower to repay his or her debt. Lenders earn profits when borrowers repay their debts. But they do not make money when borrowers default on their loans.

To figure out the chances that a borrower will default, lenders look at several factors. One of the main things that a lender examines is the borrower's credit report. A credit report has personal information such as your name, birth date, and Social Security number. It also has a credit score that shows lenders if you are a good credit risk. The score is a three-digit number, and the most common score is Fair Isaac Corporation, also known as FICO. FICO scores rate from 850 (the best) to 300 (the worst). A score of 680 or above is considered "good credit." Lenders will decide whether to loan you money based on your credit review. Your credit score will also decide what interest rate you will receive on your loan. The better your score, the lower your interest rate and cost of borrowing money.

When lenders are offering more credit, they sometimes extend credit to subprime borrowers. This group of borrowers is more likely to default on loans than the group known as prime borrowers. Subprime borrowers may have poor (or no) credit history, unpaid credit card bills, or an income that most likely does not allow for repaying the loan. They may also have FICO scores of less than 650. So why do lenders offer them credit? Lenders may give them credit because the lenders still hope to earn a profit from their loans. But when subprime borrowers start defaulting on their loans, creditors reduce their lending.

Regulated Ceilings

According to International Monetary Fund (IMF) economists Stijn Claessens, M. Ayhan Kose, and Marco Terrones, there were twenty-eight credit crunches from 1960 to 2007. During the 1960s and 1970s, the United States experienced credit crunches in 1966, 1969–1970, 1973–1974, and 1978–1981. A major factor in these crunches was that bank deposit rates had regulated ceilings. This means that banks had an upper limit on what they could offer depositors. People deposit their money in banks, and banks pay their depositors interest. But during this time, people could receive higher interest rates from other investments. So they withdrew their deposits, and banks were left with less money to lend.

Failing Banks

In the 1920s, many people borrowed money to buy cars, homes, and new appliances, including refrigerators. Then the economy fell into the Great Depression. The stock market collapsed, and banks asked borrowers to pay back their loans. When the borrowers were unable to repay their debts, banks failed. The result was a credit crisis, as banks had less money to offer and became reluctant to lend what money they did have.

Loan Defaults and Toxic Assets

Financial institutions lend money to earn profits. Borrowers who have better credit ratings receive lower interest rates on their loans. This is because these borrowers have a lower risk (chance) of defaulting on their loans. Subprime borrowers would receive higher interest rates because they have a higher chance of defaulting on their loans.

When people cannot repay their loans, banks have less money to lend. People and businesses also have less money to borrow. This leads to companies closing and more people losing work.

Lenders become risk-averse, or afraid to lend, when many borrowers begin to default on their loans. The 1999 law that allowed companies to offer banking, investment, and insurance services made lending less risky at first. This is because it allowed companies to diversify risk. Diversifying risk means that a company can balance the risk of one loan with the risk of another loan. So if a company offers a number of personal loans to prime borrowers, it may offer some home loans to subprime borrowers. Unfortunately, many of the loans given out by the financial supermarkets began to default. Afraid of losing more money, these lenders eventually stopped lending.

Another development that affected a lender's attitude toward risk was the ability to resell loans. When banks first started making loans, they held onto them until the borrowers repaid their debts. Today, lenders can resell their loans and use the money that they get from the sale to make more loans. This increases the amount of credit available. Banks can also group their debts together and sell debt packages. An asset-backed security (ABS) is a group of loans. A collateralized debt obligation (CDO) is a security that includes assets, such as loans and bonds. And a collateralized mortgage obligation (CMO) is a security that has different mortgage loans.

During the 2001–2005 credit expansion, lenders sold pieces of debt packages to other financial institutions. Think of a CDO as a pizza. Now divide the CDO into slices (called tranches) and label some of them safe investments, some of them average-risk investments, and some of them unrated risky investments. Each group has its own rate of return and risk factor. To deal with the risk, banks even sold insurance policies called credit swap defaults. Begun in the late 1990s, credit swap defaults protected the investors by guaranteeing that an asset was worthy of credit. But despite both the rating system and the credit swap defaults, many of the assets in the packages became toxic by 2006—that is, they were worth less than what the lenders paid for them. This resulted in lenders having less credit and, therefore, offering less credit.

A lender's ability to offer credit depends on two main factors. First, the lender must have available credit to offer to borrowers. Second, lenders want to feel comfortable knowing that they will get back the money that was lent, while hopefully making a profit. During the Great Depression, loan defaults and failing banks led to less available credit. In the 1960s and 1970s, regulated ceilings also left banks with less money to lend. During the recent credit crisis, the loan defaults and emergence of toxic assets resulted in less money to lend and risk-averse lenders.

Ten Great Questions
to Ask a Financial Adviser

1 How can I establish a good credit rating?

2 What happens if my bank fails during a credit crisis?

3 What are the new rules for getting a credit card?

4 What happens if I default on a loan?

5 What investments are considered "safe" during a credit crisis?

6 How will a credit crisis affect getting financial aid for college?

7 Does a credit crisis lead to a recession?

8 How do interest rates affect a credit crisis?

9 How long does a credit crisis last?

10 Will another credit crisis happen in the United States?

The Housing Crisis

At the heart of the 2007 credit crisis was the housing crisis. In 2005–2006, the price of homes started to soar. They went

In early 2009, one out of eighty-four homeowners was in danger of losing a home. By year-end, almost 25 percent owed more on their homes than what they were worth.

above what economists could explain in terms of normal supply and demand. In economics, the price and quantity of an item are usually determined by the supply of the item and its demand.

Supply is the amount of a good or service that a company is willing to offer. In the car industry, the supply may be the number of cars made by Chrysler. Demand is the amount of a good or service that people are willing and able to buy. When you buy a new pair of jeans, you are part of the demand for jeans. Both supply and demand are affected by price. Higher prices are usually associated with higher supply. This is because companies can make more money by selling their products at higher prices. Meanwhile, lower prices usually mean more demand because people are more willing and able to buy less expensive items.

Supply and demand also determine price factors such as a person's income, the prices of other homes in the area, the number of houses for sale, and how much people are willing to pay for a house. When the price of an asset drops below what can be explained by normal supply and demand factors, the asset is said to be undervalued. And when the price of an asset rises above what can be explained by normal supply and demand factors, the asset is called overvalued. By 2006, single-family homes were overvalued. In fact, homes in Naples, Florida, were overvalued by 102.6 percent.

The housing industry created a speculative bubble, which is when asset prices rise unreasonably above what is expected. And the bubble created a credit expansion. You already learned that people can use assets for collateral to take out loans. The value of your collateral partly determines how much money you can borrow. If you have a home that is worth $250,000, you can borrow more money than if your home is worth $100,000. During the housing bubble, people used their rising home values to take on more credit. When the bubble burst and home values started to drop, there was an increase in loan defaults and many of the mortgages became toxic assets. As a result, lenders had less available credit to offer.

When people cannot repay their home loans, banks take back their houses. Legally taking back collateral is called a foreclosure. From July 2007 to March 2009, 1.4 million homes were foreclosed in the United States. The hardest-hit areas were California, Florida, Arizona, and Nevada, which made up 25 percent of 2008 foreclosures. During that year, more than one million people lost their homes.

CHAPTER THREE

GROWTH OF A CREDIT CRISIS

A credit crisis is caused by a new development, such as an increase in the number of loan defaults, that eventually makes lenders stop lending. At first, lenders react to these developments by slowing down their lending and being more careful about the loans that they do make. Lenders also try to limit the amount of damage that has occurred. Finally, lenders assess the financial health of both their company and the economy to determine how much and for how long to limit lending.

Interest Rates and Leveraging

Between 1995 and 2001, an Internet, or dot-com, bubble occurred. The stocks of Internet and other technology companies became overvalued. The timing of the dot-com bubble burst and the financial consequences from the September 11, 2001, terrorist attacks prompted then-chairman of the Federal Reserve, Alan Greenspan, to lower interest rates to 1 percent in

In 2000, America Online Chairman Steve Case and Time Warner Chairman Gerald Levin announced their companies' merger. At that time, America Online had twenty million users.

order to keep the economy growing. Since interest rates are the cost of borrowing money, credit became less expensive. And when something becomes less expensive, the demand for the item usually increases. In this case, the item was credit.

Lower interest rates allowed banks to borrow money from the Federal Reserve at an even lower cost and then lend it out. But lower interest rates also meant a lower rate of return on T-bills, which encouraged investors to look elsewhere to make money. As home prices continued to rise, investors turned to the housing industry to make more money. But when housing prices started to fall, many assets became toxic and lenders stopped lending.

Leveraging is the use of borrowed money to increase the profit gained from an investment. Investors then use these profits to pay back the money that they borrowed (plus interest) and invest the extra money to make even more money. During the housing boom, many financial institutions used leverage that involved home loans to make a lot of money. They even used debt to take over other companies. This is called a leveraged buyout (LBO). But leveraging is dependent on changes in the financial and credit markets. While it can earn big profits and has tax benefits, leveraging can make financial losses even bigger. During the housing boom, some companies were borrowing $40 for every $1 they earned. But when the housing crisis hit, falling home values and loan defaults left investors with worthless assets and debts that they could not repay.

In September 2008, Fannie Mae and Freddie Mac had more than $5 trillion in debt that they could not repay. These government-sponsored companies were heavily involved in subprime lending.

Fannie Mae and Freddie Mac

According to the Fannie Mae Web site, "Fannie Mae is a government-sponsored enterprise (GSE) chartered by Congress with a mission to provide liquidity, stability and affordability to the U.S. housing and mortgage markets." Freddie Mac is also a government-chartered corporation that helps make housing more affordable by helping credit lenders stay more liquid. "Liquidity" refers to how easily a person can spend an asset. Cash is the most liquid asset.

As stated before, lenders can resell their loans. Reselling mortgage loans began with Fannie Mae and Freddie Mac. These government-sponsored companies made a secondary market for home loans, where lenders could sell mortgages to other lenders. The companies also earned a lot of money during the credit expansion years as they bought mortgages and mortgage-backed securities (investments that use buildings as collateral). Fannie Mae and

35

Freddie Mac could often obtain credit more easily than other companies because lenders had confidence in them since they were sponsored by the U.S. government.

Soon other financial institutions wanted to benefit from reselling debt packages that contained home loans. Firms started packaging adjustable rate mortgages (which are home loans where the interest rate, or cost of borrowing, changes). As firms competed with Fannie Mae and Freddie Mac, the housing industry entered the world of subprime lending. Between 2002 and 2007, Fannie Mae and Freddie Mac had made 54 percent, or $1.9 trillion, of the subprime mortgage loans. And when the housing bubble burst, Fannie Mae and Freddie Mac experienced large financial losses. In fact, in 2008, the Federal Housing Finance Agency (FHFA) believed that these government companies would soon be insolvent (unable to pay their debts).

Investment Banks Collapse

By the end of 2006, investment banks, such as Bear Stearns (the fifth-largest investment bank) and Lehman Brothers, had overextended themselves (lent too much money) and had also engaged in risky lending, such as subprime mortgages. Following the burst of the housing bubble, these banks were among the hardest hit when housing prices fell and loan defaults increased. Faced with huge financial losses, investment banks did not have the credit to offer. As a result, both consumers and banks faced a worsening credit crisis.

The eighty-five-year-old investment bank Bear Stearns was one of the first banks to become badly affected during the credit

Millions of people lost their jobs when companies like Bear Stearns failed. They took home their belongings from work in cardboard boxes.

crisis. Bear Stearns had two funds that mainly contained sub-prime mortgages. In the summer of 2007, many of these mortgages became toxic when their values fell below what investors had paid for them. Just from these funds alone, Bear

Carter Glass was one of the men who wrote the Glass-Steagall Act. This act kept banks from participating in investment activities, but it was repealed, or taken away, during the Clinton administration.

Stearns lost an estimated $1.5 billion of their investors' money. This loss forced the bank to change its lending strategy.

In addition to reducing lending by being more selective, Bear Stearns had to make sure that the public still had confi-

dence in it. After all, a lot of people had just lost their money by investing with this bank. Why should other investors keep their money with Bear Stearns? And why would new investors trust their money with Bear Stearns? Remember that financial institutions need deposits to earn profits. If a bank does not have people who trust it enough to keep their money, the bank will fail. Despite attempts to reassure investors, people pulled their money out of Bear Stearns.

Lehman Brothers was another investment bank that suffered during the credit crisis. The repeal of the Glass-Steagall Act, which allowed for financial supermarkets, low interest rates, and the housing price bubble, led to a moneymaking credit expansion for markets around the world. From 2003–2007, Lehman earned its investors almost $16 billion. But when the housing bubble burst, Lehman's investors lost a lot of money, including $350 million on real estate investments in Southern California's Inland Empire. When banks suffer huge financial losses, they do not have enough money to lend to borrowers, which worsens the credit crisis.

Financial institutions that do not have enough money to extend credit or meet their reserve requirements have liquidity problems. Banks can increase liquidity by borrowing from other banks. But even when a bank borrows money, its lender has to believe that the bank will repay the loan. In March 2008, when Bear Stearns tried to obtain a short-term $2 billion loan, another major bank said no. Even among other banks, confidence in Bear Stearns was low. Liquidity is related to confidence. If a bank is suffering from a liquidity crisis, the public will quickly lose confidence in it. This leads to investment banks fighting for their own survival and again not having credit to offer to borrowers.

As financial institutions continued to lose billions of dollars, the credit crisis grew more serious. Banks did not have excess money to lend, became more risk-averse, tried to convince the public to have confidence in them, and struggled to improve their liquidity. What began as a twenty-first century credit expansion turned into a credit crisis less than a decade later.

MYTHS and FACTS

MYTH The housing crisis did not have anything to do with the 2007 credit crisis.

FACT The housing crisis led to the 2007 credit crisis. The housing crisis consisted of a large number of loan defaults. These defaults resulted in banks and other companies losing millions—and in some cases, billions—of dollars. The large financial losses made lenders more risk-averse and left them without any money to lend.

MYTH Financial supermarkets on Wall Street made most of the subprime mortgages.

FACT Fannie Mae and Freddie Mac made more than half of the subprime mortgages from 2002–2007. These government-sponsored corporations also started the secondary market that allowed for lenders to resell home loans.

MYTH Liquidity is not related to a credit crisis.

FACT Liquid assets are used to extend credit. They are also used to assess the financial health of a bank or other company.

CHAPTER FOUR

EFFECTS OF
A CREDIT CRISIS

A credit crisis occurs when lenders stop lending money because they are afraid of risk or do not have excess cash. As the credit crisis grows, more and more people are affected by less available credit. Eventually, a credit crisis becomes a financial crisis and banks, companies, the general public, a country's economy, and the global economy are affected.

With less credit available, financial institutions begin to fail. A bank can fail because it does not have enough cash to give to its depositors or to pay its bills. Before 1933, when banks failed, people lost all of the money in their accounts. This was a major problem during the Great Depression, when nine thousand banks stopped operating between 1929 and 1933.

Since the Banking Act of 1933, most banks are insured by the Federal Deposit Insurance Corporation (FDIC), and their customers are protected. In 2008, the FDIC raised the protection limit to $250,000. This means that even if a bank fails, investors' money (up to a quarter of a million dollars) is protected.

When a bank fails, the FDIC steps in and takes over. Then the FDIC can overtake the failed bank or sell it to another bank. Either way, customers still carry out their banking transactions as usual. As the 2007 credit crisis grew into a financial crisis, FDIC protection became very important. In 2005 and 2006, the FDIC reported zero bank failures. But between 2007 and August 2009, almost one hundred banks failed.

Fannie Mae and Freddie Mac also failed during this time. These corporations had given out more than half of the subprime home mortgages. When many of their assets became toxic, Fannie Mae and Freddie Mac lost a lot of money. The government stepped in and gave them the first major bailout of

The Federal Deposit Insurance Corporation (FDIC) protects people who keep their money in banks. Even if an FDIC-insured bank fails, people will not lose all of their money.

the financial crisis. At first, these two corporations received an $85.9 billion bailout.

A bailout means a failing company is given or loaned money in hopes of saving it (or keeping it financially sound).

During the recent credit crisis, many people who worked for Michigan car companies lost their jobs. By August 2009, 1.5 million people in Michigan were out of work.

Who pays for a bailout? The taxpayers pay for bailouts. If you and your parents are working, you are among the taxpayers who pay for bailouts. If the money received from taxes is not enough to cover government expenses (including bailouts), the country's deficit grows larger and larger. This, in turn, creates a bigger debt for the country.

Other companies also received bailouts from the government during the recent credit crisis. AIG received a $180 billion bailout, after the company had zero dollars to lend or repay their debts with. Carmakers General Motors (GM) and Chrysler ended up receiving close to $50 billion through bailouts and other programs. But even with the bailout money, GM still declared bankruptcy. In other words, GM legally declared that it could not pay its debts. This led to GM being nationalized, which means that the company was taken over and run by the government.

Aside from bailouts and nationalizing companies, failing companies can be bought out by stronger financial institutions.

Bear Stearns and Lehman Brothers were in terrible financial trouble during the credit crisis. The American bank JPMorgan Chase & Company bought Bear Stearns and the U.K. bank Barclays bought Lehman Brothers.

Costs to the Public

When companies and banks go out of business, people lose their jobs. In the automotive industry, more than four hundred thousand people lost their jobs during the most recent financial crisis—that is approximately the same number of people that live in Miami, Florida. In June 2007, about seven million people were out of work. But by June 2009, more than 14.7 million people were without jobs. In other words, the number of unemployed people more than doubled in two years.

When people lose their jobs, they have a harder time affording basic needs, including food, clothing, and housing. As people struggle to pay their bills, they often default on loans, such as mortgages and credit card bills. Eventually, banks may foreclose on people's properties. This causes people to lose their homes. According to *Business Week*, more than one million people lost their homes in 2008.

During the most recent credit crisis, many of the financial supermarkets lost a lot of their investors' money. When people make investments, they are taking a chance with their money. They take a risk because they hope to make more money. But there is always a chance that they can lose their money, too. Many people invest their money to achieve goals, such as paying for college or retirement. If your parents put $1,000 into a college investment that had a 7 percent rate of return compounded quarterly (four times a year), in 10 years, that money would double. But what happens if the company that your parents invested with fails? You lose your college money and the original $1,000. During the credit crisis, many people lost their savings. Some people who had worked their whole lives and kept their money in retirement funds were suddenly left without any money to live on.

A Global Stock Market Crisis

A stock is a share of a company. When you own a stock, you own part of a company. People buy stocks because they hope to make money when the value of the stock increases. If you buy a stock for $20 and the stock's price increases to $30, you would make a $10 profit if you sold the stock.

Stocks are bought and sold every day in a stock exchange. The Dow Jones Industrial Average is a price-weighted average of the thirty American stocks that are bought and sold most often, including stocks for banks, computer companies, and restaurant corporations. The performance of the Dow Jones indicates the financial strength of both the companies that own the stocks and the economy. In the midst of the recent credit crisis, the Dow Jones suffered one of its largest point drops, falling 504 points on September 15, 2008. The next day, Moscow, Russia's largest stock exchange, suffered its largest one-day point drop in ten years. The stock exchanges in England, Germany, France, and Latin America also plunged. And Japan suffered its biggest stock market drop in history.

Recessions

When banks fail, businesses close, people lose their jobs, and the whole economy suffers. A country's gross domestic product

During a recession in July 1982, hundreds of people ran to withdraw their money from the insolvent Penn Square Bank in Oklahoma.

(GDP) refers to the market value of all goods and services produced within a country. For the United States, this number includes all products produced in any of the fifty states, the District of Columbia, and the five U.S. territories (such as Puerto Rico). A recession is a decline in real (adjusted for inflation) GDP for at least two consecutive quarters (or six months in a row).

According to the Financial Stability Oversight Board, the recessions that followed the 1969, 1973, 1981, 1991, and 2007 business cycle peaks can be called credit crunch recessions because they followed periods of reduced access to credit. During a recession, the economy is producing less goods and services. This leads to fewer available jobs, which makes it harder for unemployed people to find work. With more people out of work, consumers are spending less in the stores. This can cause stores to lower inventories (the amount of products that they keep on the shelves) and, eventually, close if they lose too much business. Lenders also become more risk-averse when the economy is weakened. They are less likely to offer credit, which makes it harder for people to afford goods and services and for businesses to grow.

A recession may also become a depression, which is a severe, prolonged recession. This was the case in 1929 at the start of the Great Depression, which followed the Roaring Twenties credit expansion. Before the recent credit crisis, the U.S. economy had grown for seventy-three months. But after the credit crisis, the National Bureau of Economic Research announced a recession that had begun in December 2007 and continued through 2008 and 2009. It was the longest recession in the United States since the 1930s.

International Consequences

This is a time of globalization. People are connected to other people around the world through computers, cell phones, and transportation. Businesses often have stores in many countries, such as McDonald's, which operates more than 31,000 restaurants in 107 countries. A business may also make parts of their products in various countries. A carmaker may design a car in one country, make the parts of the car in a second country, and assemble the car in a third country. This is an example of division of labor on an international level.

As people and businesses become connected, the economies of different countries become dependent on each other. The Japanese automaker Toyota gives jobs to Americans who live in places such as Kentucky, Indiana, and West Virginia. Likewise, people who work for McDonald's in London depend on the jobs that this American company provides. Countries also give

In Texas, many U.S. autoworkers earn their living by working for the Japanese company Toyota Motor Corporation.

credit to one another, such as when Chinese investors buy U.S. Treasury bonds.

The recent credit crisis showed just how much countries are becoming dependent on one another. According to the *London Evening Standard*, four thousand people who worked for Lehman Brothers in London lost their jobs and another one thousand people were in danger of becoming unemployed. In Japan, Bloomberg News reported an increase in the number of homeless people due to Lehman's collapse. The British Broadcasting Corporation (BBC) reported that the "global credit crisis" had begun in 2007, when both U.S. and European banks lost hundreds of billions of dollars. This led to banks around the world becoming more risk-averse and offering less credit.

Many economists also feared that the American housing crisis, credit crisis, and recession would cause a worldwide recession. An increase in the number of people without jobs and decreases in consumer spending and confidence (belief that the economy will improve) continued. On October 10, 2008, *Business Week* even reported that the country of Iceland was officially bankrupt because it was unable to repay its debts and its currency was worthless.

CHAPTER FIVE

COMING OUT OF A CREDIT CRISIS

To come out of a credit crisis, the government and the central bank try to make more money available to lenders because a crisis happens when there is not enough credit available. They also work to reduce the harmful effects of the crisis, such as unemployment. Their actions affect the public, including you and your family.

Help from the Federal Reserve

Most countries have central banks. There are 172 central banks in the world. The central bank in the United States, the Federal Reserve, has a chairman, a vice chairman, and a seven-person Board of Governors. All nine positions are chosen by the president of the United States and confirmed by the U.S. Senate.

There are twelve Federal Reserve districts that include Boston, New York, Philadelphia, Cleveland, Richmond, Atlanta, Chicago, St. Louis, Minneapolis, Kansas City, Dallas, and San Francisco. Each bank services a region. For example, the

Ben S. Bernanke is the chairman of the Federal Reserve. In 2009, he said, "The world is suffering through the worst financial crisis since the 1930s [Great Depression]."

Federal Reserve Bank in Minneapolis provides services to Minnesota, North Dakota, South Dakota, Montana, parts of northwestern Wisconsin, and Michigan's Upper Peninsula. The Board of Governors is located in Washington, D.C.

The Federal Reserve has several important jobs. First, the central bank influences the growth of the money supply and the credit market. Second, the Fed tries to manage risk in the financial markets. Third, it oversees the banking institutions to protect the customers and keep a healthy banking system. Finally, the Fed provides banking services, such as making loans, to other banks, the U.S. government, and other countries.

To come out of a credit crisis, the Federal Reserve needs to make more credit available. It can do this in four ways. First, the Fed can lower interest rates by increasing the growth of the money supply. Since interest is the cost of borrowing money, banks can now receive credit at a lower cost and then offer more credit to consumers.

The Federal Funds Rate and Monetary Policy

The Federal Reserve affects the price of credit by determining an interest rate called the federal funds rate. This is the interest rate that depository institutions, such as banks, charge when they lend money to each other. Banks borrow at one rate and then charge a higher interest rate on the loans that they make. So the federal funds rate influences the profit that a bank can earn on a loan. And the more money that a bank lends out, the more money it can potentially earn. But banks cannot loan out all of their money because they need to meet their reserve requirements.

The Fed influences the money supply and determines interest rates through open market operations. The central bank buys and sells securities, mostly government bonds and T-bills. When the Fed sells securities, it decreases the money supply and raises interest rates. This makes less credit available. But when the Fed buys securities, it increases the money supply and lowers interest rates. This makes more credit available.

To help the country come out of the recent credit crisis, the Fed pumped a lot of money into the economy by buying U.S. Treasury bonds, mortgage-related bonds, corporate debt, and consumer loans. This lowered the overnight federal funds rate to the lowest level in history, ranging from 0 to 25 percent. The central bank even made new lending programs for businesses and consumers and suggested new rules to protect people applying for mortgages.

The second thing that the Fed can do to affect the amount of available credit is change the reserve requirements. If the requirement is lowered, the banks have more credit to offer to their customers.

Third, there is something called contractual clearing balances, which are the amounts that a bank may need to keep at the Federal Reserve Bank in addition to its reserve requirement. Lowering this would also give banks more money to lend. Finally, the Federal Reserve has discount window lending, which allows depository institutions to receive credit extensions through other programs. When the Fed influences the growth of the money supply to affect the economy, it is using monetary policy.

The Federal Government Steps In

The federal government may also take steps to make more credit available during a credit crisis. In addition, the government works to reduce the harmful effects of the crisis, including those that arise from a recession. A government uses two actions of fiscal policy—government spending and tax measures—to help the economy. This is called economic stimulus.

A country's GDP includes government expenses. When a government builds new roads, it helps the economy by increasing the GDP. It also creates jobs. When people have jobs, they use their paychecks to buy food, pay their rents or mortgages, and other living expenses. This helps the people who own food stores, apartment houses, and other businesses. The new employees also deposit their paychecks into banks, which the banks can then use to make loans. Increasing government

In March 2009, President Obama said that the $787 billion stimulus package would make or protect 150,000 jobs in the road-building industry by the end of 2010.

expenditures can create jobs, put more money into the economy, and encourage people to spend money.

Taxes are another tool that the government can use to help boost the economy. When a person works, part of the money that he or she earns is given to the government in the form of taxes. If there is a reduction in the tax rates (also known as a tax cut), people have more money to spend because less of their earnings are going to taxes. When consumers spend more money, this helps a country's economy grow. A government can also give tax rebates to increase consumer spending. A tax rebate is a refund, or money received back, from the government when a person or business pays too much in taxes.

The federal government used both tools of fiscal policy to deal with the recent credit crisis. In February 2008, a $168 million economic stimulus bill was passed under the Bush administration. This package included tax rebates for more than one hundred million low-income and middle-income Americans and tax breaks for businesses. The government hoped that the tax breaks would encourage businesses to expand and create more jobs.

A year later, President Barack Obama signed the American Recovery and Reinvestment Act into law. This act was the largest government spending in history. According to the White House, the $787 billion act provided tax breaks for 95 percent

President Obama hoped that the American Recovery and Reinvestment Act would help the economy recover from the recession and the credit crisis.

of American workers and their families. The economic stimulus package also included tax breaks for college students, first-time homeowners, new car owners, and people who make energy-saving home improvements. Part of the act was a $150 billion investment in infrastructure, such as improving and building bridges and roads. The act was intended to save and create about 3.5 million jobs from 2009 to 2011.

Both the Federal Reserve and the federal government worked to lessen the effects of the recent housing crisis, credit crisis, and recession. Together, they spent, lent, or agreed to give $12.8 trillion to boost the economy. This amount was more than the 2005 GDP.

CHAPTER SIX

CAN CREDIT CRISES BE AVOIDED?

Credit crises happen in countries around the world. Economists and politicians have different opinions on how to avoid a credit crisis and how to recover from one. When economists study economic activity, they analyze many scenarios, models, graphs, and statistics. They also come up with many different answers. In fact, President Harry Truman once said, "Give me a one-handed economist. All my economists say, 'On the one hand, on the other.'"

Avoiding Bubbles

In 1593, tulips were brought over from Turkey to Holland. People thought that the flower was so beautiful, an increase in demand drove up its price. Then the flower caught a virus that gave the petals a colorful "flame" pattern. This made the flowers even more desirable, and the price of the flowers continued to rise. The result was a speculative bubble in the tulip industry.

Soon people were even trading their savings and land for tulips. Eventually, the price of the flowers fell and the bubble burst.

A similar lesson could be learned from the 2006 American housing crisis. The speculative bubble in housing contributed to the recent credit expansion. Increasing housing prices encouraged people to borrow a lot, which resulted in huge financial losses when the housing prices fell. The burst of the housing industry bubble meant that many people and companies could not repay their debts. This led to the recent credit crisis.

Speculative bubbles, or very large increases in the price of an asset, lead to rising stock markets. But when the bubble bursts, stock markets fall.

Some economists suggest that bursting a speculative bubble might help avoid a credit crisis. However, it is difficult to both identify and burst a bubble in time. This was the case in the 1980s, when the Bank of Japan kept interest rates low to boost their economy. Lower interest rates led to a lot of available cheap credit. Bubbles arose in both the real estate and stock markets.

According to Nariman Behravesh, the chief economist for IHS Global Insight, "Between 1986 and 1989, equity and land prices more than doubled," and "companies and households borrowed heavily on the basis of the rise in asset values." But when the Bank of Japan raised interest rates, it burst the bubble, which "led to a 60 percent drop in the Japanese stock market and a 70 percent drop in property prices over the next four years." A credit crisis followed as banks were faced with loan defaults, and Japan suffered one of its worst recessions.

Stress Tests

The Obama administration wanted to assess whether the leading U.S. banks would survive an even weaker economy. The administration created a "stress test," which was given to nineteen banks. The stress test asked the banks to figure out what would happen if the economy weakened, including a rise in unemployment to 10.3 percent, a drop in housing prices by 2.2 percent, and GDP growth of negative 3.3 percent. Some people who study the financial markets (also known as financial analysts) and economists worried that the tests presented an economic scenario that was too optimistic.

The results of the stress tests came in May 2009. They indicated that ten out of the nineteen banks would need more money to survive another economic downturn. In fact, CNN Money reported that an additional $75.6 billion was needed. The nine banks that passed the test included American Express, Capital One Financial Corporation, Goldman Sachs, Bank of New York Mellon Corporation, and JPMorgan Chase & Company. These banks also began repaying their Troubled Asset Relief Program (TARP) money in June 2009.

Creating New Regulations

There is a group of economists and politicians who feel that more regulations, or rules, will help prevent a future credit crisis. They believe that the deregulation that allowed for the financial supermarkets made the credit crisis worse. They also are aware of the harmful effects of lightly regulating investments, such as hedge funds.

On June 16, 2009, President Obama said that he believed the financial crisis was due in part to a lack of regulation, or government oversight. Since then, his administration has proposed new regulations for many industries, including banks, carmakers, and credit card companies. These regulations include allowing stockholders to influence executives' pay, regulating hedge funds, pushing certain investment tools (such as derivatives) to be traded publicly, making firms keep a part of the home loans that they sell, and giving the federal government the right to take control of a large company that is failing if that failure threatens the U.S. economy.

President Obama also proposed creating a consumer financial protection agency that would regulate mortgages, set credit card fees, limit or prohibit risky lending, and protect credit card users. On May 22, 2009, he signed a credit card bill into law. The bill prohibits credit card companies from raising interest rates on customers who are less than sixty days late on a payment, and it prohibits them from offering credit cards to people under twenty-one without a parent's permission or a plan to pay. It also restricts penalty fees, such as late fees.

It is uncertain what effects an increase in regulations would have on the present credit crisis or a future one. Regulating the

When President Obama took office, one of his top goals was to fix the economy. But, he warned Americans that an economic recovery was "not going to happen overnight."

financial system is a constant topic of debate among economists. Supporters of regulation feel that the credit crisis happened in part because of not enough regulation, while opponents of too much regulation can cite a recent International Monetary Fund study as evidence that regulation is not always the answer. The study found that some of the worst financial crises have occurred in countries, such as Japan, that have a lot of financial regulations.

Improving Balance Sheets

People decide if a bank or corporation is financially sound by looking at its balance sheet. A balance sheet shows the financial condition of a business at a certain time. It lists assets, liabilities, and owners' equity. Assets are items of value, such as cash, a building, and equipment. Liabilities are things that a company owes (its debts), such as loans. Owners' equity is the amount invested in the company by the owners. When a balance sheet is balanced, assets equal liabilities, plus owners' equity. But if a business's liabilities are greater than its assets, the company owes more than it owns.

In September 2008, another phase of the credit crisis occurred as the economy worsened. In the short run, the Federal Reserve and the federal government helped banks to increase their available credit by lowering interest rates (the price of credit) and increasing their liquid assets (the amount of credit). But for banks to survive harsh economic conditions and still be able to have enough liquid assets to provide credit, banks need to be solvent. This means that the banks' assets are greater than their liabilities.

To help banks became solvent, the Bush administration created the Troubled Asset Relief Program (TARP), which was

FINANCIAL STABILITY and RECOVERY

Secretary of the Treasury Timothy Geithner discusses the government plan to improve the economy, including taking over toxic assets and reducing the number of foreclosures.

part of the Emergency Stabilization Act of 2008. TARP gave the secretary of the treasury the authority to buy troubled assets, such as subprime mortgages, from financial institutions. The Treasury worked with both the Federal Reserve and the FDIC to help banks clean up their balance sheets. President Obama said that he hoped these actions would help families "get basic consumer loans, auto loans, student loans, [so] that small businesses are able to finance themselves, and we can start getting this economy moving again."

The recent credit crisis changed the financial landscape. Financial supermarkets failed, were bought out, or taken over by the government. Major corporations were nationalized, and the stock market has still not hit pre-crisis levels. The country is facing one of the longest recessions in U.S. history. Many Americans have lost their savings, are struggling to keep their homes, and are unable to pay their credit card bills. The credit crisis has had many harmful effects. But credit crises have happened before, and countries survive and continue to thrive.

GLOSSARY

asset Something of value to its owner.

bankruptcy A legal situation where a borrower is unable to pay his or her creditor.

collateral A physical asset that may be taken away if the borrower is unable to pay his or her debt.

credit Borrowing money to pay for an expense.

credit cycle A series of expansions (where more money is available to lend) and contractions (where less money is available to lend) in available credit.

creditor Someone who lends money to be repaid in the future.

debt Something that is borrowed and needs to be repaid.

default Failure to meet the requirements of a loan.

deficit Amount of money overspent in a specific period of time.

federal funds rate Interest rate that depository institutions, such as banks, charge when they lend money to each other.

Federal Reserve Central bank in the United States.

fiscal policy Actions by the government that affect the economy, including government spending and tax measures.

interest Cost of borrowing money.

investment Use of money to try and make more money.

liquidity The availability of liquid assets, such as cash, to a company or market.

loan Borrowed money to be repaid under certain conditions.

monetary policy Actions by the central bank that affect the economy by managing the money supply.

regulation Rules for private-sector businesses, such as credit card companies.

risk Chance of something turning out differently than anticipated.

speculative bubble When the price of an asset rises above what normal economic conditions can explain.

subprime borrower Someone with a poor credit history who takes on credit.

FOR MORE INFORMATION

Bank of Canada
Public Information
234 Wellington Street
Ottawa, ON K1A 0G9
Canada
(613) 782-8111
Web site: http://www.bank-banque-canada.ca
The Bank of Canada is Canada's central bank. Its duties include
  conducting monetary policy, issuing bank notes (money), and
  facilitating transactions that promote a stable financial system.

Board of Governors of the Federal Reserve System
20th Street and Constitution Avenue NW
Washington, DC 20551
Web site: http://www.federalreserve.gov
The Federal Reserve is the United States' central bank. Its use
  of monetary policy, through the Federal Open Market
  Committee, affects the economy.

Department of the Treasury
1500 Pennsylvania Avenue NW
Washington, DC 20220
(202) 622-2000
Web site: http://www.ustreas.gov/organization

The Department of the Treasury is a government organization that has many duties, including collecting taxes, managing public debt, supervising national banks, and advising the president on economic issues.

Equifax
P.O. Box 740241
Atlanta, GA 30374-0241
(800) 685-1111
Web site: http://www.equifax.com/home
Equifax is one of the three major credit reporting agencies in the United States. It provides credit reports to consumers, including FICO scores, and helps with identity theft.

Experian
P.O. Box 9595
Allen, TX 75013-9595
(888) 397-3742
Web site: http://www.experian.com
Experian is one of the three major credit reporting agencies in the United States. It provides credit reports to consumers and helps with identity theft.

Federal Deposit Insurance Corporation (FDIC)
Public Information Center
3501 North Fairfax Drive
Arlington, VA 22226
(877) 275-3342
Web site: http://www.fdic.gov
This government corporation insures deposits in many depository institutions, such as banks, for at least $250,000.

TransUnion
P.O. Box 1000
Chester, PA 19022
(800) 888-4213
Web site: http://www.transunion.com
TransUnion is one of the three major credit reporting agencies in the United States. It provides credit reports to consumers and helps with identity theft.

Treasury Board of Canada Secretariat
Strategic Communications and Ministerial Affairs
L'Esplanade Laurier, 9th Floor, East Tower
140 O'Connor Street
Ottawa, ON K1A 0R5
Canada
(877) 636- 0656
Web site: http://www.tbs-sct.gc.ca
This Canadian government body oversees financial management responsibilities in federal departments and agencies.

Web Sites

Due to the changing nature of Internet links, Rosen Publishing has developed an online list of Web sites related to the subject of this book. This site is updated regularly. Please use this link to access the list:

http://www.rosenlinks.com/rwe/cred

FOR FURTHER READING

Aliber, Robert, Charles P. Kindleberger, and Robert Solow. *Manias, Panics, and Crashes: A History of Financial Crises.* Hoboken, NJ: Wiley Publishing, 2005.

Browning, Richard. *How to Survive the Credit Crunch.* Winchester, England: Studio Cactus, 2008.

Bucci, Steve. *Credit Repair Kit for Dummies.* Hoboken, NJ: Wiley Publishing, 2008.

Calverley, John. *When Bubbles Burst: Surviving the Financial Fallout.* Boston, MA: Nicholas Brealey Publishing, 2009.

Garber, Peter M. *Famous First Bubbles.* Boston, MA: The MIT Press, 2001.

Hollander, Barbara. *Managing Money.* Chicago, IL: Heinemann Library, 2009.

Howard, Laura, Simon Read, and Annie Read. *100 Ways to Beat the Credit Crunch.* London, England: Flame Tree Publishing, Ltd., 2008.

Jones, Brian T. *Getting Started: The Financial Guide for a Younger Generation.* Potomac, MD: Larstan Publishing, Inc., 2006.

Kansas, Dave. *Guide to the End of Wall Street as We Know It.* New York, NY: Collins & Brown, 2009.

Kelly, Kate. *Street Fighters: The Last 72 Hours of Bear Stearns, the Toughest Firm on Wall Street.* New York, NY: Portfolio Hardcover Publishing, 2009.

King, Peter. *Housing Boom and Bust: Owner Occupation, Government Regulation and the Credit Crunch.* New York, NY: Routledge, 2010.

Kochan, Nick, and Hugh Pym. *What Happened? And Other Questions Everyone Is Asking About the Credit Crunch.* London, England: Old Street Publishing, Ltd., 2005.

Nixon, Simon. *The Credit Crunch: How Safe is Your Money?* London, England: Pocket Issue, 2008.

Porterfield, Jason. *How a Depression Works.* New York, NY: Rosen Publishing, 2010.

Stutely, Richard. *Guide to Economic Indicators, Making Sense of Economics.* 6th ed. New York, NY: Bloomberg Press, 2007.

Tilson, Whitney, and Glenn Tongue. *More Mortgage Meltdown: 6 Ways to Profit in These Bad Times.* Hoboken, NJ: Wiley Publishing, 2009.

Weiss, Martin. *The Ultimate Depression Survival Guide: Protect Your Savings, Boost Your Income, and Grow Wealthy Even in the Worst of Times.* Hoboken, NJ: Wiley Publishing, 2009.

BIBLIOGRAPHY

Andrews, Wyatt. "What Does a Bank 'Stress Test' Entail?" CBS Evening News, February 25, 2009. Retrieved July 2009 (http://www.cbsnews.com/stories/2009/02/25/eveningnews/main4829645.shtml).

Andriotis, Annamarie. "Banks Lowering Consumers' Credit-Card Limits." SmartMoney, September 2008. Retrieved July 2009 (http://www.smartmoney.com/spending/deals/banks-lowering-consumer-credit-card-limits).

Behravesh, Natiman. *Spin-Free Economics*. New York, NY: McGraw-Hill, 2009.

Bishop, Matthew. *Essential Economics: An A-Z Guide*. 2nd ed. New York, NY: Bloomberg Press, 2009.

Boyd, Roddy. "The Last Days of Bear Stearns." CNNMoney.com, March 31, 2008. Retrieved July 2009. (http://www.money.cnn.com/2008/03/28/magazines/fortune/boyd_bear.fortune).

Boyle, Catherine. "US Banks Borrow Record Amount from Fed." TimesOnline, October 3, 2008. Retrieved July 2009 (http://www.business.timesonline.co.uk/tol/business/industry_sectors/banking_and_finance/article4872458.ece).

Bruner, Robert F., and Sean D. Carr. *The Panic of 1907, Lessons Learned from the Market's Perfect Storm.* Hoboken, NJ: Wiley Publishing, 2007.

Budworth, David. "The Credit Crunch Explained." TimesOnline, June 11, 2009. Retrieved June 2009 (http://www.timesonline.co.uk/tol/money/reader_guides/article4530072.ece).

Carey, Mark, Stephen Prowse, John Rea, and Gregory Udell. "The Economics of the Private Placement Market." The Federal Reserve System, December 1993. Retrieved July 2009 (http://www.federalreserve.gov/pubs/staffstudies/1990-99/ss166.pdf).

Cohen, Joshua, Joel Rogers, and Juliet Schor. *Do Americans Shop Too Much?* Boston, MA: Beacon Press, 2000.

College Board. "Trends in Student Aid 2008." Retrieved July 2009 (http://www.salliemae.com/NR/rdonlyres/CD5EDF04-324D-430A-90B9-FF599ECB93D2/10167/TheCollegeBoard_Trends_in_student_aid_2008.pdf).

Cooper, George. *The Origin of Financial Crisis.* New York, NY: Vintage Books, 2008.

Federal Reserve System. "Purposes and Functions." 2005. Retrieved July 2009 (http://www.federalreserve.gov/pf/pdf/pf_complete.pdf).

FinancialStability.gov. "U.S. Credit Cycles: Past and Present." 2009. Retrieved August 2009 (http://www.financialstability.gov/docs/CPP/Report/Fed%20US%20Credit%20Cycles%20072409.pdf).

Isidore, Chris. "Fannie & Freddie: The Most Expensive Bailout." CNNMoney.com, July 27, 2009. Retrieved August 2009

(http://www.money.cnn.com/2009/07/22/news/
companies/fannie_freddie_bailout/index.htm?
section=money_latest).

Ivry, Bob, and Mark Pittman. "Financial Rescue Nears GDP
as Pledges Top $12.8 Trillion." Bloomberg.com,
March 31, 2009. Retrieved June 2009 (http://http://
www.bloomberg.com/apps/news?pid=20601087&sid=
armOzfkwtCA4&refer=worldwide).

Lee, Jesse. "A New Era for Credit Cards." WhiteHouse.gov,
May 25, 2009. Retrieved July 2009 (http://www.
whitehouse.gov/blog/A-New-Era-for-Credit-Cards).

Lindstrom, Martin. *Buyology*. New York, NY: Doubleday, 2008.

Maltby, Emily. "Restarting the Frozen Loan Market."
CNNMoney.com, January 15, 2009. Retrieved July
2009 (http://www.money.cnn.com/2009/01/08/
smallbusiness/smallbiz_loans_talf.smb/index.htm).

Mandel, Michael. "Iceland Goes Bankrupt." *BusinessWeek,*
October 10, 2008. Retrieved July 2009 (http://www.
businessweek.com/the_thread/economicsunbound/
archives/2008/10/iceland_goes_ba.html).

McGeever, Jamie, and John Parry. Reuters. "Banks Borrowing
from Fed Reaches Record $188 Billion a Day."
August 25, 2008. Retrieved August 2009 (http://
www.gata.org/node/6679).

Michaelson, Adam. *The Foreclosure of America*. New York, NY:
Berkeley Books, 2009.

New York Times. "Credit Crisis—The Essentials." July 17,
2009. Retrieved June 2009 (http://www.topics.
nytimes.com/topics/reference/timestopics/subjects/c/
credit_crisis).

Newman, Rick. "9 Bailout Surprises from GM and Chrysler." *U.S. News & World Report,* February 18, 2009. (http://www.usnews.com/blogs/flowchart/ 2009/02/18/9-bailout-surprises-from-gm-and- chrysler.html).

Palmeri, Chris. "Over One Million People Lost Their Home in 2008." *BusinessWeek,* January 14, 2009. Retrieved July 2009 (http://www.businessweek.com/the_thread/ hotproperty/archives/2009/01/over_one_millio.html).

Solomon, Deborah. "Nine Banks to Repay TARP Money." *Wall Street Journal.* Retrieved July 2009 (http://www. online.wsj.com/article/SB124450458046896047.html).

Sowell, Thomas. *The Housing Boom and Bust.* New York, NY: Basic Books, 2009.

Turner, Graham. *The Credit Crunch: Housing Bubbles, Globalisation and the Worldwide Economic Crisis.* London, UK: Pluto Press, 2008.

Woods, Thomas E., Jr. *Meltdown.* Washington, DC: Regnery Publishing, Inc., 2009.

INDEX

About the Author

Barbara Gottfried Hollander received her B.A. in economics from the University of Michigan and her M.A. in economics, specializing in statistics and econometrics, from New York University. She is the author of *Paying for College*, *Managing Money*, and *Raising Money* and both the Economics and Education Editor of the *2009 World Almanac and Book of Facts*. She also develops, writes, and reviews business and mathematics course material for Knowledge Learning Corporation.

Photo Credits

Cover (top) © www.istockphoto.com/Lilli Day; cover (bottom), p. 1 © Shutterstock; p. 9 © John Nordell/Image Works; pp. 10–11 © Scott Olson/Getty Images; p. 14 © www.istockphoto.com/Marcia Clarkson; pp. 18–19 © www.istockphoto.com; pp. 24–25 © Dorothea Lange/FPG/Hulton Archives/Getty Images; pp. 28–29 © Ethan Miller/Getty Images; pp. 32–33 © Stan Honda/AFP/Getty Images; pp. 34–35, 43 © Karen Bleier/AFP/Getty Images; pp. 37, 48–49 © AP Images; pp. 38–39 Library of Congress Prints and Photographs Department; pp. 44–45 © John Gress/Reuters/Landov; p. 51 © San Antonio Express–News/Zuma Press; p. 54 © Ryan Kelly/Getty Images; p. 57 © www.istockphoto.com/Mike Clarke; p. 58 www.colorado.gov; p. 61 © www.istockphoto.com/Bjorn Meyer; p. 64 © Win McNamee/Getty Images; p. 66 © J. Richards/AFP/Getty Images.

Designer: Sam Zavieh; Editor: Karolena Bielecki;
Photo Researcher: Marty Levick